Guess What!

Student's Book 2

American English

Susannah Reed with Kay Bentley

Series Editor: Lesley Koustaff

CAMBRIDGE
UNIVERSITY PRESS

Contents

3

Hello again!

Guess What!

1 (CD1 03) Listen. Who's speaking?

2 (CD1 04) Listen, point, and say.

1 Ben   2 Olivia   3 David   4 Tina

5 Leo

3 (CD1 05) Listen and find.

Find Leo

Say the chant.

(sister)

This is my sister.
Her name's Olivia.
How old is she?
She's eight.

(brother)

(friend)

(friend)

 Find the mistakes and say.

Number 1. His name's Ben. He's eight.

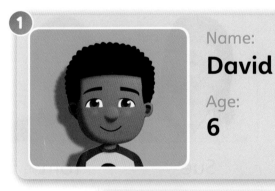
Name: **David**
Age: **6**

Name: **Tina**
Age: **7**

Name: **Ben**
Age: **5**

Name: **Olivia**
Age: **9**

6 CD1 08 **Sing the song.**

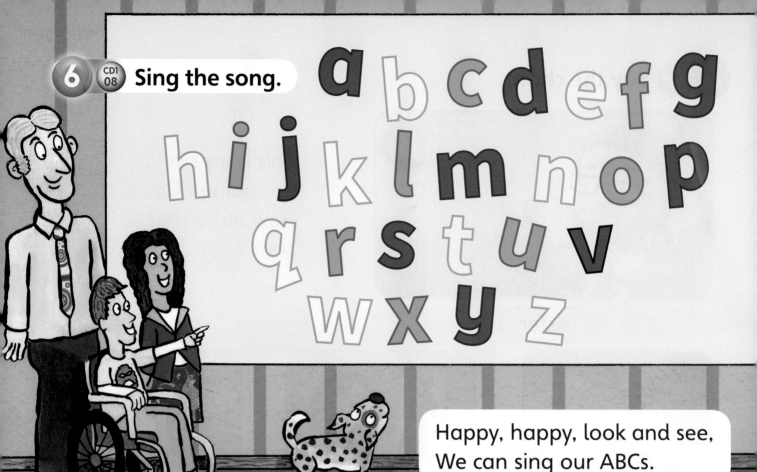

Happy, happy, look and see,
We can sing our ABCs.

7 CD1 09 **Listen and point.**

Dan   Jill   Sam   Sue   Tom

8 About Me **Ask and answer.**

What's your name?   My name's Harry.

How do you spell "Harry"?   It's H-A-R-R-Y.

9 CD1 11 Listen, look, and say.

1 What's this?

It's a ruler.

2 What are these?

They're books.

10 CD1 12 Listen and point.

11 Ask and answer.

b, 1. What's this?

It's a red bike.

Grammar: *What's this?*   **9**

1. This is our tree house.

We have a surprise for you!

2. Stand here. You hold iPal.

3. This is iPal.

Hello, Ben! Let's play.

4. Do you like animals?

Yes, I do.

5. ROAR!

Oh, dear! Help!

Don't worry.

6. Wow! What a big surprise!

And look, Ben! Your lion!

Value: Play together

→ Workbook page 8

13   **Listen and act.**

Animal sounds

14 CD1 16 Listen and say.

The rabbit can run. The lion is lazy.

What kind of **art** is it?

1 🔊 CD1 18 Listen and say.

photography   drawing   sculpture   painting

2 Watch the video.

3 Look and say the kind of art.

Number 1. Sculpture.   Yes.

Guess What!

Project

4 Make a class sculpture.

1 Transportation

Guess What!

1 (CD1 19) Listen. Who's speaking?

2 (CD1 20) Listen, point, and say.

1 plane

2 helicopter

3 bus

4 car

5 truck

6 motorcycle

7 train

8 boat

9 tractor

3 (CD1 21) Listen and find.

Find Leo

Say the chant.

car

This is my car.
It's a big red car.
This is my car,
And it goes like this.
Vroom! Vroom!

bike

train

boat

5 Match and say.

Number 1, c . It's a tractor!

  Ask and answer.

Do you like motorcycles? Yes, I do.

→ Workbook page 13

17

7 CD1 24 **Sing the song.**

I have a ,
You have a .
He has a ,
And she has a .

Let's play together.
Let's share our toys.
Let's play together.
All the girls and boys.

I have a ,
You have a .
He has a ,
And she has a .

Let's play together …

I have a ,
You have a .
He has a ,
And she has a .

Let's play together …

8 CD1 25 **Listen and say the name.**   She has a train.   May.

Tim

May

Alex

Lucy

9 CD1 27 **Listen, look, and say.**

Does he have a plane?

Yes, he does.

Does she have a plane?

No, she doesn't. She has a car.

10 CD1 28 **Look and match. Then listen and answer.**

Number 1. Does she have a ball?   No, she doesn't.

11 **Ask and answer.**

Number 1. Does she have a ball?   No, she doesn't.

Grammar: *Does he have a plane?* **19**

1. Ben has a helicopter!
   Let's go to the park!

2. Does Ben have a robot?
   No, he doesn't. It's a helicopter.

3. Can I have a turn, please?
   Yes, of course!

4. Thank you. This is fun!
   Be careful, iPal!

5. Sorry. Now let's play with my helicopter!
   It's OK.

6. Wow! The helicopter is iPal!

13   **Listen and act.**

Animal sounds

14  **Listen and say.**

A gorilla on the grass. A hippo in the house.

Where is the transportation?

1 CD1 34 Listen and say.

on land

on water

in the air

2 Watch the video.

3 Look and say *on land, on water,* or *in the air.*

Number 1. On land.   Yes.

Guess What!

Project

4 Find transportation on land, on water, and in the air.

on land   On Water   in the air

2 Pets

Guess What!

1 CD1 35 Listen. Who's speaking?

2 CD1 36 Listen, point, and say.

1 woman

2 man

Pet Show

3 girl

4 cat

5 mouse

6 fish

7 boy

8 dog

9 baby

10 frog

3 CD1 37 Listen and find.

Find Leo

→ Workbook page 20

4 CD1 38 **Say the chant.**

mice

fish

One frog, two frogs.
Big and small.
Come on now, let's count them all.
One, two, three.
Three green frogs.

dogs

frogs

5 **Look, find, and count.** I can see two women.

women

men

babies

children

  6 About Me **Look at your classroom. Then say.** I can see five boys.

7 **CD1 40** **Listen, look, and say.**

1

2 ugly

beautiful

3

old

4

young

5 happy

6 sad

7 big

8 small

8 **CD1 41** **Listen, find, and say.**

They're cats.

They're happy.

9 **Make sentences. Say *yes* or *no*.**

Number 1. It's a bird. It's ugly.

No. It's beautiful.

10 CD1 42 **Sing the song.**

I'm at the pet store.
I'm at the pet store.
Can you guess which
pet is my favorite?

Is it small? No, it isn't.
Is it big? Yes, it is.
Is it beautiful? No, it isn't.
Is it ugly? Yes, it is.
It's big and ugly.
Let me guess, let me
guess. Oh, yes!
It's a fish! It's a fish!

I'm at the pet store.
I'm at the pet store.
Can you guess which
pets are my favorites?

Are they old? No, they aren't.
Are they young? Yes, they are.
Are they sad? No, they aren't.
Are they happy? Yes, they are.
They're young and happy.
Let me guess, let me guess. Oh, yes!
They're dogs! They're dogs!

11 Think **Play the game.**

Is it happy? No it isn't.

Is it a dog? Yes, it is!

Are they beautiful? No, they aren't.

Are they spiders? Yes, they are!

1

Look! What's that?

It's a frog!

2

It's Aunt Sue! Hello.

Oh, dear! She's sad.

3

Can we help?

MISSING

Yes, please. I can't find my cat.

4

Mr. Tom. He's big … and he's beautiful!

What's his name?

MISSING

5

What's that?

6

Thank you.

You're welcome!

13   **Listen and act.**

Animal sounds

14 **Listen and say.**

A fox with a fish. A vulture with vegetables.

What do animals need?

1 **CD1 49** **Listen and say.**

water

food

shelter

2 **Watch the video.**

3 **Look and say *water*, *food*, or *shelter*.**

Number 1. Water.   Yes!

Guess What!

Project

4 **Draw a home for a pet.**

Review Units 1 and 2

1 Look and say the words. Number 1. Bus.

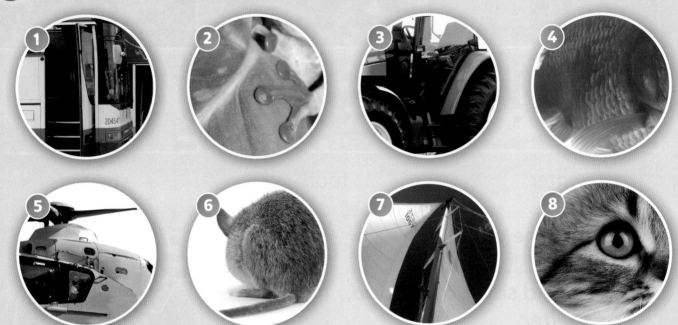

2 CD1 50 Listen and say the color.

Tony

Anna

May

Bill

Play the game.

What's this? / What are these?	How do you spell ... ?	What does he/she have?	Is he / Are they ... ?
1	2	3	4

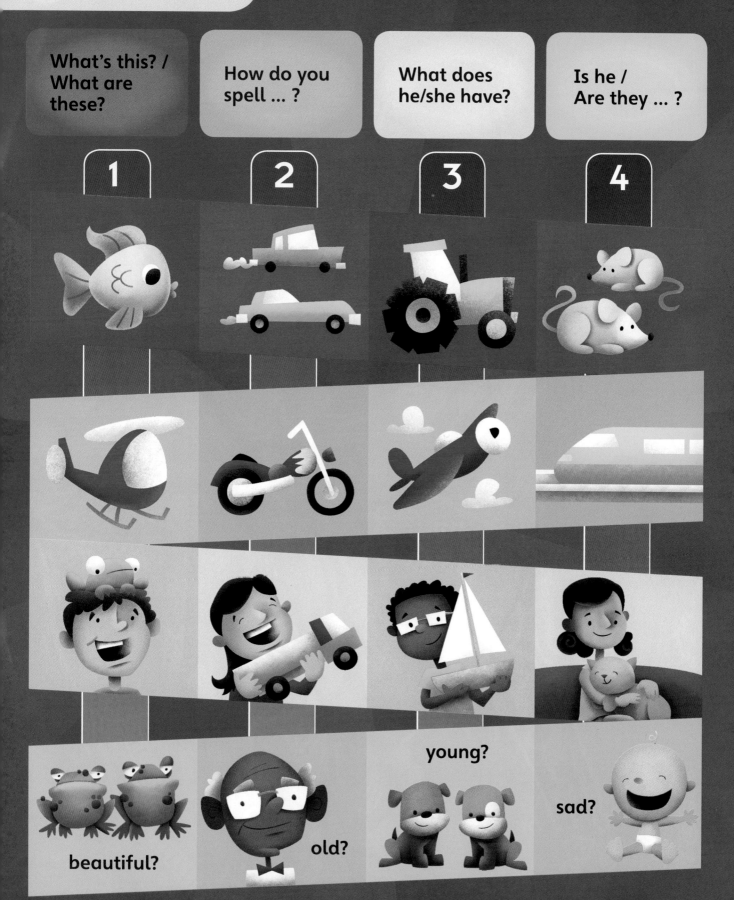

beautiful?

old?

young?

sad?

35

3 Clothes

Guess What!

1 (CD1 52) **Listen. Who's speaking?**

2 (CD1 53) **Listen, point, and say.**

1 jacket

2 pants

3 socks

5 shoes

4 skirt

6 dress

7 T-shirt

8 jeans

9 shirt

3 (CD1 54) **Listen and find.**

Find Leo

→ Workbook page 30

4 CD1 55 Say the chant.

red jacket

green T-shirt

purple shoes

blue pants

Here's your jacket,
Your favorite red jacket.
Put on your jacket,
Let's go out and play.

Here are your shoes,
Your favorite purple shoes.
Put on your shoes,
Let's go out and play.

5 Think Find the mistakes and say.

His T-shirt isn't red. It's yellow.

Her shoes aren't orange. They're red.

6 (CD1 57) **Sing the song.**

What are you wearing?
What are you wearing?
What are you wearing today?

I'm wearing red
And a green .
I'm wearing a blue
And a yellow .
Oh! I look great today!

I'm wearing blue
And an orange .
I'm wearing a green
And a purple .
Oh! I look great today!

7 (CD1 58) (Think) **Listen and say the name.**

Sammy

Sally

8 (About Me) **Ask and answer.**

What are you wearing today?

I'm wearing a blue skirt.

9 CD1 59 **Listen, look, and say.**

1 Are you wearing a blue T-shirt?

Yes, I am.

2 Are you wearing brown shoes?

No, I'm not.

10 CD1 60 **Listen and point. Then play the game.**

Pink. Pants.
Are you wearing pink pants?

No, I'm not. My turn!

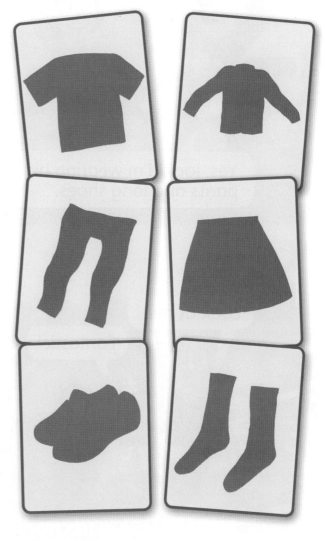

Grammar: *Are you wearing a blue T-shirt?* **41**

1

Look at these clothes!
Here's a hat for you!

2

What are you wearing?
They're clothes for a party!

3

A party?
Yes, look! I'm wearing big pants and long shoes.

4

Here you are, iPal. You can use my hat.
Thank you
And my jacket.

5

Look at me!
Fantastic!

6

First prize … The robot!
Thanks. But I'm not a robot!

42   Value: Share things

→ Workbook page 34

Listen and act.

Animal sounds

13 **Listen and say.**

Jackals don't like jello. Yaks don't like yogurt.

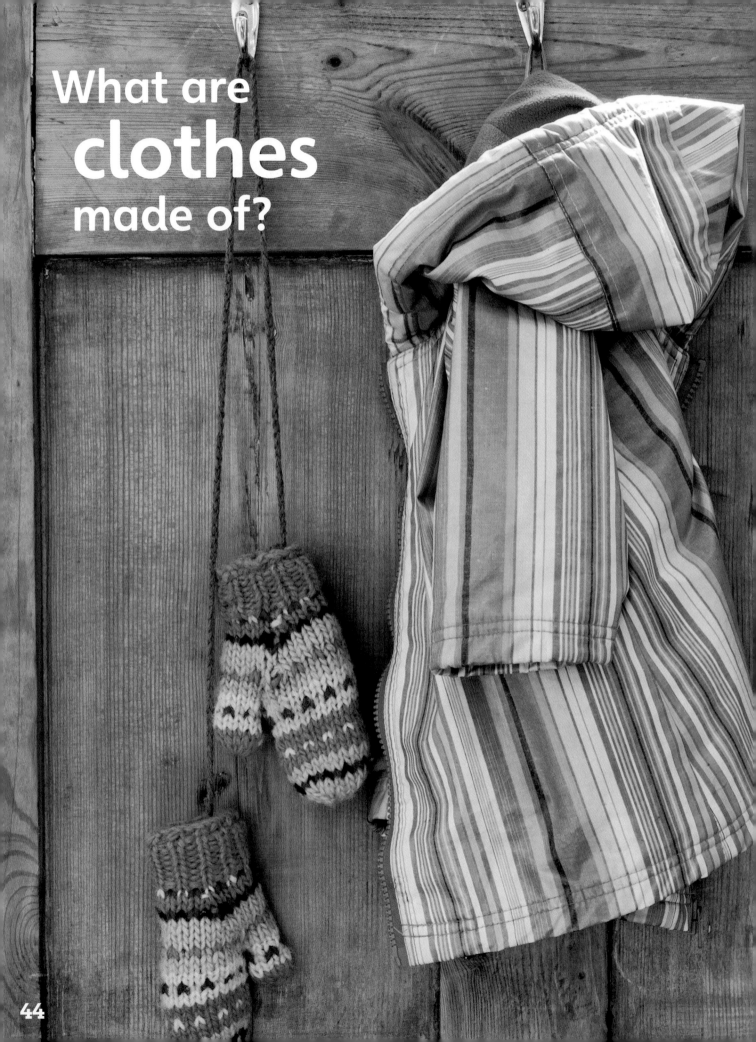

What are
clothes
made of?

1 CD1 67 Listen and say.

cotton   silk   leather   wool

2 Watch the video.

3 Look and say the material.

Number 1. Wool.   Yes!

Guess What!

Project

4 Make a collage of clothes from different countries.

Clothes

→ Workbook page 36

④ Rooms

Guess What!

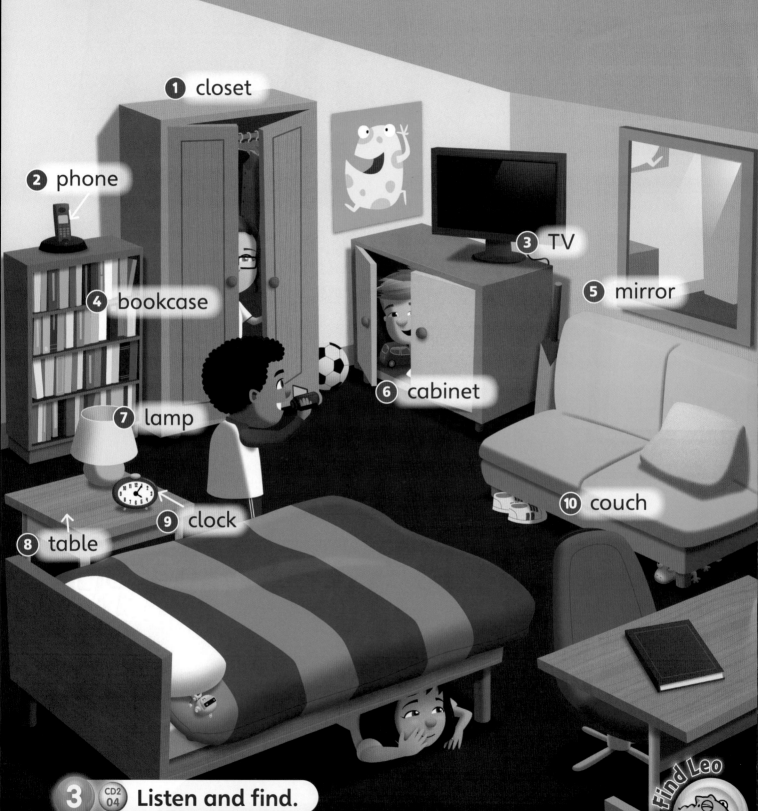

1 closet

2 phone

3 TV

4 bookcase

5 mirror

6 cabinet

7 lamp

9 clock

8 table

10 couch

Find Leo

3 CD2 04 **Listen and find.**

4 **CD2 05** **Say the chant.**

Is the lamp on the table?
Yes, it is. Yes, it is.
The lamp's on the table.

Are the books in the bookcase?
Yes, they are. Yes, they are.
The books are in the bookcase.

lamp

bookcase

clock

closet

5 **Look, ask, and answer.**

Is the phone on the bookcase?

No, it isn't. It's on the table.

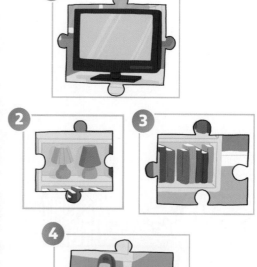

1

2 **3**

4
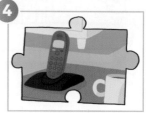

6 **What's in your bedroom? Think and say.**

My computer
is on my desk.

→ Workbook page 39

Vocabulary **49**

It's moving day, it's moving day,
And everything's wrong
on moving day.

There's a 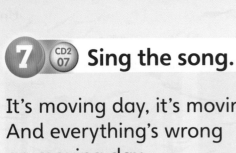 in the bathroom.
There's a in the hallway.
There's a in the kitchen.
And I can't find my ball today!

It's moving day ...

There are four s in the yard.
There are two s on my bed.
There are three s on the couch.
And where is baby Fred?

It's moving day ...

9 CD2 09 **Listen, look, and say.**

10 CD2 10 **Listen, count, and answer the questions.**

How many fish are there?

Seventeen!

11 Think **Play the game.**

There are three spiders.   No!

Grammar: *How many books are there?*

CD2 11 **Listen and read.**

Value: Be neat

→ Workbook page 42

13 (CD2 13) *Talk Time* **Listen and act.**

Animal sounds

14 (CD2 14) **Listen and say.**

Meerkats have mouths. Newts have noses.

→ Workbook page 43   Functional language: *Let's clean up!*   Pronunciation: *m, n*   **53**

How **many** are there?

1 CD2 16 **Listen and say.**

1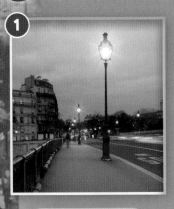
2
3
4

streetlight   bus stop   mailbox   traffic light

2 **Watch the video.**

3 **Look and say the number.**

How many streetlights are there?

There are fourteen.

Guess What!

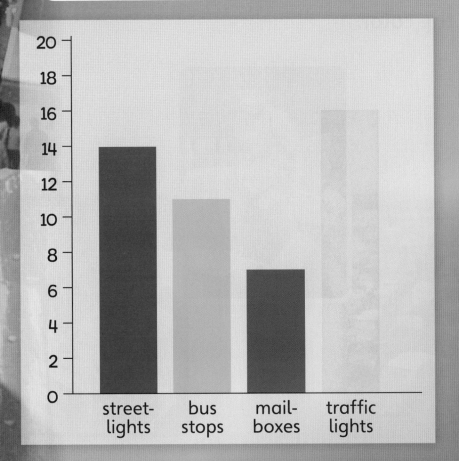

Project

4 **Make a bar chart.**

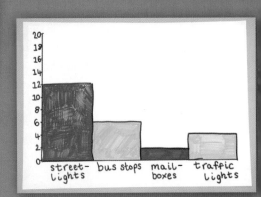

Review Units 3 and 4

1 Look and say the words.

> Number 1. Jeans.

2 CD2 17 Listen and say the color.

③ Play the game.

Finish

Are you wearing a 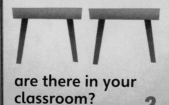 ? **17**

How many  are there in your house? **18**

Are you wearing a  ? **19**

GO BACK ONE! **20**

MISS A TURN! **16**

How many  are there in your bathroom? **15**

Are you wearing a  ? **14**

How many  are there in your classroom? **13**

Are you wearing a  ? **9**

How many are there in your kitchen? **10**

Are you wearing  ? **11**

GO BACK ONE! **12**

GO FORWARD ONE! **8**

How many  are there in your living room? **7**

Are you wearing  ? **6**

How many  are there in your bedroom? **5**

Are you wearing  ? **1**

How many 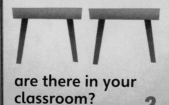 are there in your classroom? **2**

Are you wearing a  ? **3**

MISS A TURN!

Start

Meals

Guess
What!

1 CD2 19 **Listen. Who's speaking?**

2 CD2 20 **Listen, point, and say.**

The Caf...
Breakfast 8–1...
Lunch 12–...
Dinner 4–...

3.65

1 potatoes
2 carrots
3 rice
4 peas
5 sausages
6 fish
7 meat
8 beans
9 toast
10 cereal

3 CD2 21 **Listen and find.**

Find Leo

4 CD2 22 **Say the chant.**

(breakfast)

Do you like toast for breakfast?
Do you like cereal, too?
Toast and cereal for breakfast?
Yum! Yes, I do.

(lunch)

(dinner)

 5 Think **Read, look, and say. What's missing?**

Shopping list

cereal

sausages

meat

peas

potatoes

beans

rice

fish

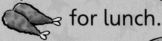 **Sing the song.**

My friend Sammy likes
 for lunch.
He doesn't like ,
And he doesn't like .
He likes and ,
And he likes .

Munch, Sammy.
Munch your lunch!

My friend Sally likes
 for lunch.
She doesn't like ,
And she doesn't like .
She likes and ,
And and .

Munch, Sally.
Munch your lunch!

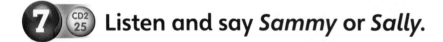

7 CD2 25 **Listen and say *Sammy* or *Sally*.**

8 About Me **Ask and answer. Then say.**

Do you like fish?

Yes, I do.

Alex likes fish.

9 (CD2 27) Listen, look, and say.

1

2

10 (Think) Ask and answer.

Tony

Kim

Is it a boy or a girl?

It's a boy.

Does he like meat?

Yes, he does.

Does he like carrots?

No, he doesn't.

It's Tony!

Tom

Pat

→ Workbook page 51

Grammar: *Does he like cereal?* **63**

11 🔊 CD2 28 **Listen and read.**

1

Look! Café Hawaii!

Café Hawaii

Let's go for lunch!

2 Café Hawaii

Would you like fish and potatoes?

Yes, please!

No, thank you!

3

What about carrots or peas, iPal?

No, thank you!

4

Oh, dear! What would you like, iPal?

Cake! I like chocolate cake.

5

More cake, please!

No, iPal. That's enough!

6

What's the matter?

He likes chocolate cake – a lot!

64   Value: Eat healthy food

→ Workbook page 52

12   **Listen and act.**

Animal sounds

13 (CD2 31) **Listen and say.**

A seal in the sun. A zebra in the zoo.

What kind of **food** is it?

1 CD2 33 Listen and say.

fruit   vegetables   meat   grains   dairy

2 Watch the video.

3 Look and say what kind of food it is.

Number 1. Fish.   Yes.

Guess What!

Project

4 Make a food poster.

fruits and vegetables   meat and fish

dairy   grains and cereals

6 Activities

Guess What!

69

1 (CD2 34) **Listen. Who's speaking?**

2 (CD2 35) **Listen, point, and say.**

Activity Day What can you do?

1. play tennis
2. play field hockey
3. play basketball
4. roller-skate
5. play baseball
6. ride a horse
7. fly a kite
8. take photographs

TODAY!

3 (CD2 36) **Listen and find.**

Find Leo

4 CD2 37 **Say the chant.**

I can play tennis.
I can't play field hockey.
Let's play tennis.
Good idea!

basketball

baseball

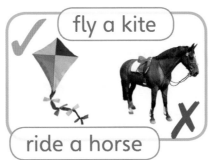

fly a kite

ride a horse

take photographs

roller-skate

5 About Me **Match and say.**

1, e. I can roller-skate.

1 I can roller-skate.
2 I can take photographs.
3 I can ride a horse.
4 I can play tennis.
5 I can play field hockey.

a

b

c

d

e

6 About Me **Point and tell your friend.**

Picture b. I can play tennis.

Picture e. I can't roller-skate.

7 (CD2 39) **Listen, look, and say.**

1. I like playing basketball, I don't like swimming.

2. I like swimming. I don't like playing basketball.

8 (CD2 40) **Listen and say the name.**

Ann

Pam

Jack

Bill

Alex

Grace

9 **Things you like. Think and say.**

I like painting.   He likes painting.

10 CD2 41 Sing the song.

Do you like ?
No, I don't. No, I don't.
Do you like ?
Yes, I do. Yes, I do.
I like !

Does he like ?
No, he doesn't. No, he doesn't.
Does he like ?
Yes, he does. Yes, he does.
He likes !

Do you like ?
No, I don't. No, I don't.
Do you like ?
Yes, I do. Yes, I do.
I like !

Does she like ?
No, she doesn't. No, she doesn't.
Does she like ?
Yes, she does. Yes, she does.
She likes !

11 CD2 42 Think Listen and say the number.

1

2

3

4

5

6

Grammar: *Do you like flying a kite?* **73**

1

Are you OK, David?

It's a basketball!

2

The *All Stars* are my favorite team!

Let's play! Put on these shirts!

3

HOME 25 GUEST 25

That's not fair!

Play nicely, iPal.

4

I'm sorry.

That's OK.

5

HOME 25 GUEST 25

Watch me! Throw the ball like this.

Yes!

6

HOME 27 GUEST 25

Good job, Olivia!

Thanks, iPal.

74 Value: Play nicely

→ Workbook page 60

13   **Listen and act.**

Animal sounds

14 CD2 46 **Listen and say.**

**A camel with
a camera.
A kangaroo
with a kite.**

What **equipment** do we need?

1 CD2 48 **Listen and say.**

①
②
③
④

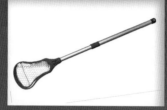

rackets   sticks   bats   balls

2 **Watch the video.**

3 **Look and say** *racket*, *stick*, *bat*, or *ball*.

Number 1. Ball.   Yes!

Guess What!

Project

4 **Make a Carroll diagram.**

Review Units 5 and 6

1 Look and say the words.

Number 1. Fly a kite.

2 CD2 49 Listen and say the color.

Sue

Dan

→ Workbook pages 64–65

3 Play the game.

Do you like ?

Does he like ?

18 Do you like ?

Finish

15 Does she like ?

14 Do you like ?

13 Does he like ?

12 Do you like ?

Does she like ?

8 Do you like ?

Does he like ?

9 Do you like ?

11

10

7 Does she like ?

6 Do you like ?

Does he like ?

5 4 Do you like ?

3 Does she like ?

Start

1 Does he like ?

2 Do you like ?

79

7 In town

Guess What!

1 CD3 02 Listen. Who's speaking?

2 CD3 03 Listen, point, and say.

1 park

2 movie theater

MOVIE THEATER

Now Showing: Robots From Outer Space

3 clothing store

4 café

5 toy store

6 bookstore

7 supermarket

8 street

9 school

10 playground

Cozy Café

The Toy Store

The Toy Store

Bert's Books

The Clothing Store

Supermarket

Beans Get 1 Free

Coffee 30% Off

SCHOOL

Find Leo

3 CD3 04 Listen and find.

4 CD3 05 Say the chant.

Come with me and look around.
Who's in the café in the town?
It's my sister! She's in the café.
She's in the café in the town.

sister

brother

mom

dad

5 Match and say.

1, c. My cousin's on the playground.

a

b

1 My cousin's on the playground.
2 My aunt's in the clothing store.
3 My uncle's in the school.
4 My grandma's in the supermarket.
5 My grandpa's at the park.

c

d

e

6 Think Think of a place. Say and guess.

There's a desk and green chairs.

It's a school.

7 CD3 07 **Sing the song.**

Come and visit my town,
My friendly little town.
It's nice to be in my town,
My little town.

There's a toy store and
a clothing store.
There's a bookstore
and a movie theater.
There's a café, and
there's a supermarket.
In my little town.

And the toy store is behind the
clothing store.
And the bookstore is in front of
the clothing store.
And the clothing store is between
the bookstore and the toy store!
In my little town.

And the movie theater is next to the café.
And the café is next to the supermarket.
And the café is between the supermarket
and the movie theater.

Come and visit my town …

8 CD3 08 **Look, listen, and find the mistakes.**

> The movie theater is next to the supermarket.

> No, it isn't. The movie theater is next to the café.

Listen, look, and say.

Is there a playground behind the school?

Yes, there is.

Is there a café next to the movie theater?

No, there isn't.

 Listen and say *yes* or *no*.

  Play the game.

Is there a café in front of the supermarket?

Yes, there is.

The movie theater is next to the school.

No, it isn't. The movie theater is next to the supermarket.

Grammar: *Is there a playground behind the school?*

1 Movie tickets!

They're from my cousin, Anna!

2 MOVIES

Where's the movie theater?

SUPERMARKET

It's next to the supermarket.

3 Let's go!

No, iPal! Be careful!

4 Look left and right.

It's safe now. Let's cross.

5 Oh, no! It's closed today!

NOW SHOWING

The Queen

Come with me!

6 It's a movie about robots!

I like going to the movies.

86   Value: Be safe

13 CD3 13 Talk Time **Listen and act.**

Animal sounds

14 CD3 14 **Listen and say.**

A quick queen bee. An ox with an X-ray.

Where are the places?

1 CD3 16 Listen and say.

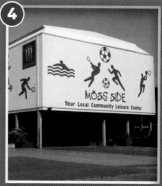

police station   fire station   hospital   sports center

2 Watch the video.

3 Look and say the letter and number.

A, 3.   Fire station.   Yes!

Guess What!

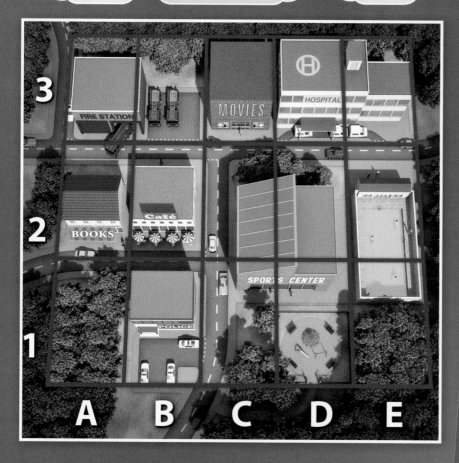

Project

4 Draw a map of your town.

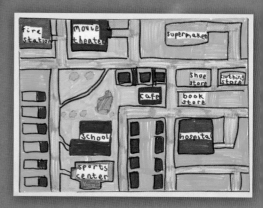

8 On the farm

1 (CD3 17) Listen. Who's speaking?

2 (CD3 18) Listen, point, and say.

Café and Gift Store

1 field

2 barn

3 horse

4 donkey

5 sheep

6 goat

7 cow

8 duck

3 (CD3 19) Listen and find.

9 pond

Find Leo

4 CD3 20 Say the chant.

donkey

Where's the donkey?
It's in the barn.
It's in the barn.
On the farm.

Where are the goats?
They're in the field.
They're in the field.
On the farm.

cow

goats

ducks

5 Read and follow. Then ask and answer.

Where's the cow?   It's in the field.

a

1 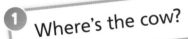 Where's the cow?

2 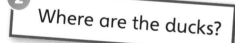 Where are the ducks?

b

3 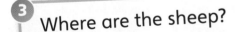 Where are the sheep?

4 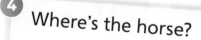 Where's the horse?

c

6 About Me Ask and answer.

What's your favorite animal?   It's a sheep.

7 (CD3 22) **Sing the song.**

Field and pond, house and barn,
Look at the animals on the farm …

What's the doing?
It's swimming. It's swimming.
It's swimming.
What's the doing?
It's swimming in the .

Field and pond …

What's the doing?
It's running. It's running. It's running.
What's the doing?
It's running in the .

Field and pond …

What's the doing?
It's sleeping. It's sleeping.
It's sleeping.
What's the doing?
It's sleeping in the .

Field and pond …

What's the doing?
It's eating. It's eating. It's eating.
What's the doing?
It's eating in the .

Field and pond …

8 (CD3 23) **Listen and answer the questions.**

What's the duck doing?   It's swimming.

1
2
3
4
5
6
7
8

9 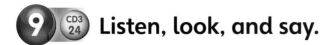 **Listen, look, and say.**

1 Is the cat sleeping?   Yes, it is.

2 Is the duck swimming?   No, it isn't. It's flying.

10 Think **Play the game.**

Is the dog running?

Yes, it is.

Picture 1!

Grammar: *Is the cat sleeping?* **95**

1. It's a message for iPal.
   Let's find him!

2. Would you like to come to a party?
   Yes, please!

3. Hold on!
   We're flying!

4. Welcome to the party!
   It's so nice to see you!
   WELCOME HOME

5. What's Ben doing?
   He's ... dancing!

6. Goodbye, iPal!
   Goodbye! Thanks for taking care of me!

96 | Value: Love your home

→ Workbook page 78

12   **Listen and act.**

Animal sounds

13 (CD3 29) **Listen and say.**

A wolf in the water.
A white whale with a wheel.

Functional language: *Would you like to come to my party?*
Pronunciation: *w, wh*   **97**

What do **farmers** do?

1 CD3 31 **Listen and say.**

1 plant seeds

2 turn soil

3 water plants

4 harvest plants

2 **Watch the video.**

3 **Look and say.**

Number 1. He turns soil.   Yes!

Guess What!

1

2

3

4

Project

4 Draw how farmers grow our food.

Review Units 7 and 8

1 Look and say the words.

Number 1. Café.

2 CD3 32 Listen and say the name.

Grace

Lola

Kento

Dan

→ Workbook pages 82–83

3 Ask and answer.

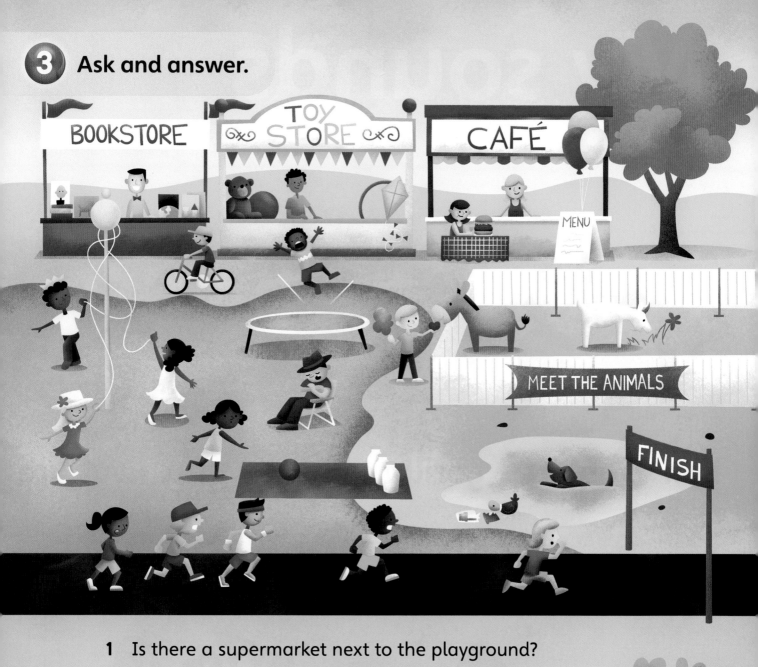

1 Is there a supermarket next to the playground?

2 What is between the bookstore and the café?

3 Is there a pond at the park?

4 What is the duck doing?

5 Is the dog sleeping?

6 What is the donkey doing?

7 Is she eating cereal?

8 What's he doing?

9 Is she swimming?

10 What's he doing?

My sounds

lion • rabbit

gorilla • hippo

fox • vulture

jackal • yak

meerkat • newt

seal • zebra

camel • kangaroo

queen bee • ox

wolf • whale

Thanks and Acknowledgments

Many thanks to everyone in the excellent team at Cambridge University Press. In particular we would like to thank Emily Hird, Liane Grainger, and Flavia Lamborghini whose professionalism, enthusiasm, experience, and talent makes them all such a pleasure to work with.

We would also like to give special thanks to Lesley Koustaff for her unfailing support, expert guidance, good humor, and welcome encouragement throughout the project.

The authors and publishers would like to thank the following contributors:

Blooberry Design: concept design, cover design, book design, page makeup
Emma Szlachta: editing
Lisa Hutchins: freelance editing
Ann Thomson: art direction, picture research
Gareth Boden: commissioned photography
Jon Barlow: commissioned photography
Ian Harker: audio recording
Robert Lee, Dib Dib Dub Studios: song and chant composition
Vince Cross: theme tune composition
James Richardson: arrangement of theme tune
John Marshall Media: audio recording and production
Phaebus: video production
hyphen S.A.: publishing management, American English edition

The authors and publishers acknowledge the following sources of copyright material and are grateful for the permissions granted. Although every effort has been made, it has not always been possible to identify the sources of all the material used or to trace all copyright holders.

If any omissions are brought to our notice, we will be happy to include the appropriate acknowledgments on reprinting.

The authors and publishers would like to thank the following illustrators:
Bill Bolton, pp41; Marek Jagucki, pp5, 6, 7, 10, 15, 16, 20, 25, 26, 30, 37, 38, 42, 47, 48, 52, 59, 60, 64, 69, 70, 74, 81, 82, 86, 91, 92, 96; Kirsten Collier (Bright Agency), pp11, 21, 31, 43, 53, 65, 75, 87, 97, 102, 103; Andy Parker, pp39, 89; Phil Garner (Beehive Illustration), pp17, 27; Joelle Dreidemy (Bright Agency), pp27, 61, 83; Woody Fox (Bright Agency), pp8, 18, 29, 40, 50, 62, 73, 84; Richard Watson (Bright Agency), pp28, 41, 51, 63, 95; Chris Jevons (Bright Agency), pp51; Marcus Cutler (Sylvie Poggio), pp35, 57, 79, 101; Gareth Conway, pp49

The authors and publishers would like to thank the following for permission to reproduce photographs:

p.2–3: Galyna Andrushko/shutterstock; p.4–5: Images Etc Ltd/Getty Images; p.8 (Dan): Valua Vitaly/Shutterstock; p.8 (Jill): Jacek Chabraszewski/Shutterstock; p.8 (Sam): Monkey Business Images/Shutterstock; p.8 (Sue): Lorelyn Medina/Shutterstock; p.8 (Tom): michaeljung/Shutterstock; p.9 (CL): AnnalA/Shutterstock; p.9 (C): terekhov igor/Shutterstock; p.9 (CR): Wil Tilroe-Otte/Shutterstock; p.9 (BL): Gena73/Shutterstock; p.9 (BC): incamerastock/Alamy; p.9 (BR): Mikhail Olykaynen/Alamy; p.11 (B/G), p.32 (B/G), p.43 (B/G), p.53 (B/G), p.75 (B/G): Tim Jackson/Getty Images; p.12: Robin Weaver/Alamy; p.13 (1): scyther5/Shutterstock; p.13 (2): Chukcha/Shutterstock; p.13 (3): veryan dale/Alamy; p.13 (4): Africa Studio/Shutterstock; p.13 (CL): Serge Vero/Shutterstock; p.13 (CR): Matej Kastelic/Shutterstock; p.13 (BL): Corbis; p.13 (BC): MaKars/Shutterstock; p.14–15: Guido Cozzi/Corbis; p.17 (1), p.17 (c), p.34 (3): Argentieri/Getty Images; p.17 (2); p.17 (d): Philip Lange/Shutterstock; p.17 (3); p.17 (b): Margo Harrison/Shutterstock; p.17 (4); p.17 (a): John Orsbun/Shutterstock; p.19 (a): Scott Rothstein/Shutterstock; p.19 (b): V. J. Matthew/Shutterstock; p.19 (c): s oleg/Shutterstock; p.19 (d): Aprilphoto/Shutterstock; p.19 (e): Mikael Damkier/Shutterstock; p.21 (B/G): SZE FEI WONG/Getty Images; p.22–23: imageBROKER/Alamy; p.23 (TL): Buzz Pictures/Alamy; p.23 (TC): David Fowler/Shutterstock; p.23 (TR): Dwight Smith/Shutterstock; p.23 (CL): Bailey-Cooper Photographer/Alamy; p.23 (C): antb/Shutterstock; p.23 (CR): Dhoxax/Shutterstock; p.23 (1): Andrey Pavlov/Shutterstock; p.23 (2): Elena Elisseeva/Shutterstock; p.23 (3): Patrick Foto/Shutterstock; p.23 (4): maxpro/Shutterstock; p.24–25: antos777/Getty Images; p.27 (men): Viorel Sima/Shutterstock; p.27 (women): stockyimages/Shutterstock; p.27 (babies): StockLite/Shutterstock; p.27 (children): Gelpi JM/Shutterstock; p.32–33: SurangaSL/Shutterstock; p.33 (TL): Barna Tanko/Shutterstock; p.33 (TC): g215/Shutterstock; p.33 (TR): Tierfotoagentur/Alamy; p.33 (CL): J Reineke/Shutterstock; p.33 (C): skynetphoto/Shutterstock; p.33 (CR): Galyna Andrushko/Shutterstock; p.33 (2): David Sucsy/Getty Images; p.33 (3): BarbarosKARAGULMEZ/Getty Images; p.33 (4): Vitaly Titov & Maria Sidelnikova/Shutterstock; p.34 (1): DWD-photo/Alamy; p.34 (2): shane partdridge/Alamy; p.34 (4): Mikael Damkier/Shutterstock; p.34 (5): paul prescott/Shutterstock; p.34 (6): Tsekhmister/Shutterstock; p.34 (7): Olga Bogatyrenko/Shutterstock; p.34 (8): DenisNata/Shutterstock; p.34 (Tony): MANDY GODBEHEAR/Shutterstock; p.34 (Anna): Judy Kennamer/Shutterstock; p.34 (May): Victoria Blackie/Getty Images; p.34 (BL): Willyam Bradberry/Shutterstock; p.34 (BC dog):

Matthew Williams-Ellis/Shutterstock; p.34 (BC mice): Geoffrey Lawrence/Shutterstock; p.34 (BR): DreamBig/Shuttrstock; p.36–37: Bartosz Hadyniak/Getty Images; p.39 (TL): Mo Peerbacus/Alamy; p.39 (TR): artproem/Shutterstock; p.39 (CL): Zoonar GmbH/Alamy; p.39 (CR): Irina Rogova/Shutterstock; p.44–45: Tim Gainey/Alamy; p.45 (T-1): THPStock/Shutterstock; p.45 (T-2): Sofiaworld/Shutterstock; p.45 (T-3): smereka/Shutterstock; p.45 (T-4): Randy Rimland/Shutterstock; p.45 (cotton): pixbox77/Shutterstock; p.45 (silk): Tramont_ana/Shutterstock; p.45 (leather): illustrart/Shutterstock; p.45 (wool): trossofoto/Shutterstock; p.45 (B-1): Lucy Liu/Shutterstock; p.45 (B-2): Picsfive/Shutterstock; p.45 (B-3): karkas/Shutterstock; p.45 (B-4): Gulgun Ozaktas/Shutterstock; p.45 (B-5): Loskutnikov/Shutterstock; p.46–47: LeeYiuTung/Getty Images; p.49 (TL): LianeM/Getty Images; p.49 (TR): donatas1205/Shutterstock; p.49 (CL): akud/Shutterstock; p.49 (CR), p.56 (B): Image Source/Alamy; p.53 (T): Datacraft – QxQ images/Alamy; p.54–55, p.89 (3): Justin Kase zsixz/Alamy; p.55 (1): Radius Images/Alamy; p.55 (2): Taina Sohlman/Shutterstock; p.55 (3): Jack Sullivan/Alamy; p.55 (4): stocker1970/Shutterstock; p.56 (1): Teerasak/Shutterstock; p.56 (2): Kitch Bain/Shutterstock; p.56 (3): Marek Uszynski/Shutterstock; p.56 (4): Pearlimage/Alamy; p.56 (5): Africa Studio/Shutterstock; p.56 (6): Chukcha/Shutterstock; p.56 (7): Nolte Lourens/Shutterstock; p.56 (BL): Bart Broek/Getty Images; p.58–59: Naho Yoshizawa/Shutterstock; p.63 (Tony): Craig Richardson/Alamy5; p.63 (Kim): Tracy Whiteside/Alamy; p.63 (Tom): Blend Images/Alamy; p.63 (Pat): Tracy Whiteside/Alamy; p.63 (meat): Jacek Chabraszewski/Shutterstock; p.63 (fish): Eskymaks/Shutterstock; p.63 (potatoes): Kevin Mayer/Shutterstock; p.63 (carrots): Maria Komar/Shutterstock; p.63 (rice): oriori/Shutterstock; p.63 (beans): mayer kleinostheim/Shutterstock; p.63 (toast): alnavegante/Shutterstock; p.65 (B/G), p.97 (B/G): Jolanta Wojcicka/Shutterstock; p.66 (T): Andrew Olney/Shutterstock; p.66–67: Stefano Politi Markovina/Alamy; p.67 (T-1): matka_Wariatka/Shutterstock; p.67 (T-2): sarsmis/Shutterstock; p.67 (T-3): Jag_cz/Shutterstock; p.67 (T-4): Christine Langer-Pueschel/Shutterstock; p.67 (T-5): Christian Draghici/Shutterstock; p.67 (B-1): koss13/Shutterstock; p.67 (B-2): Christian Jung/Shutterstock; p.67 (B-3): Adam Gault/Getty Images; p.67 (B-4): Africa Studio/Shutterstock; p.68–69: Leander Baerenz/Getty Images; p.71 (baseball): Dan Thornberg/Shutterstock; p.71 (basketball): Aaron Amat/Shutterstock; p.71 (kite): Hurst Photo/Shutterstock; p.71 (horse): Alex White/Shutterstock; p.71 (camera): taelove7/Shutterstock; p.71 (skates): J. Helgason/Shutterstock; p.71 (a): gorillaimages/Shutterstock; p.71 (b): Veronica Louro/Shutterstock; p.71 (c): Ramona Heim/Shutterstock; p.71 (d): Rob Bouwman/Shutterstock; p.72 (C): Hybrid Images/Getty Images; p.72 (CR): Production Perig/Shutterstock; p.72 (C): racorn/Shutterstock; p.72 (BL): auremar/Shutterstock; p.72 (BR): Kuttig - People/Alamy; p.75 (T): F1online digitale Bildagentur GmbH/Alamy; p.76–77: 13/David Madison/Ocean/Corbis; p.77 (T-1); p.77 (T-2): Image Source Plus/Alamy; p.77 (T-3): onilmilk/Shutterstock; p.77 (T-4): Aaron Amat/Shutterstock; p.77 (rackets): anaken2012/Shutterstock; p.77 (sticks): Bill Frische/Shutterstock; p.77 (bats): Sean Gladwell/Shutterstock; p.77 (balls): mexrix/Shutterstock; p.77 (B-1): Pal2iyawit/Shutterstock; p.77 (B-2): Ian Buchan/Shutterstock; p.77 (B-3): isitsharp/Getty Images; p.77 (B-4): Visionhaus/Corbis; p.78 (1): Fir4ik/Shutterstock; p.78 (2): Ledo/Shutterstock; p.78 (3): Nattika/Shuterstock; p.78 (4): Ramon grosso dolarea/Shutterstock; p.78 (5): Tischenko Irina/Shutterstock; p.78 (6): igor.stevanovic/Shutterstock; p.78 (7): Joe Gough/Shutterstock; p.78 (8): Elnur/Shutterstock; p.78 (Sue): Tracy Whiteside/Shutterstock; p.78 (Dan): oliveromg/Shutterstock; p.78 (BC skates): StockPhotosArt/Shutterstock; p.78 (BC hockey): Leonid Shcheglov/Shutterstock; p.78 (BL): Igor Dutina/Shutterstock; p.78 (BR): Lauri Patterson/Getty Images; p.80–81: Peter Burnett/Getty Images; p.83 (TL): Gladskikh Tatiana/Shutterstock; p.83 (brother): Pavel L Photo and Video/Shutterstock; p.83 (mom): racorn/Shutterstock; p.83 (dad): Carlos Yudica/Shutterstock; p.87 (B/G): AAMNF3/Alamy; p.87 (T): Adrian Sherratt/Alamy; p.88: A.P.S.(UK)/Alamy; p.89 (1): meunierd/Alamy; p.89 (2): Sava Alexandru/Getty; p. 89 (3): Rosalrene Betancourt 5/Alamy; p.89 (4): Mike Robinson/Alamy; p.90–91: Getty Images; p.93 (TL): Dieter Hawlan/Shutterstock; p.93 (TR): Orhan Cam/Shutterstock; p.93 (CL): Sebastian Knight/Shutterstock; p.93 (a): American Spirit/Shutterstock; p.93 (b): Scott Prokop/Shutterstock; p.93 (c): Brian Goodman/Shutterstock; p.94 (B/G): Dudarev Mikhail/Shutterstock; p.94 (horse): Lenkadan/Shutterstock; p.94 (field): robert_s/Shutterstock; p.94 (duck): Geanina Bechea/Shutterstock; p.94 (pond): Yuriy Kulik/Shutterstock; p.94 (cat): Rumo/Shutterstock; p.94 (house): bbofdon/Shutterstock; p.94 (cow): jesadaphorn/Shutterstock; p.94 (barn): Bonita R. Cheshier/Shutterstock; p.94 (1): Diane Picard/Shutterstock; p.94 (2): Schubbel/Shutterstock; p.94 (3): Ewa Studio/Shutterstock; p.94 (4): Michael Durham/Getty Images; p.94 (5): Makarova Viktoria/Shutterstock; p.94 (6): Kemeo/Shutterstock; p.94 (7): Ballawless/Shutterstock; p.94 (8): Alexander Matvienko/Alamy; p.98–99: Stephen Dorey/Getty Images; p.99 (1): Danylo Saniylenko/Shutterstock; p.99 (2): Tim Scrivener/Alamy; p.99 (3): Keith Dannemiller/Corbis; p.99 (4): Alex Treadway/National Geographic Society/Corbis; p.100 (1): Shchipkova Elena/Shutterstock; p100 (2): Arterra Picture Library/Alamy; p.100 (3): THPStock/Shutterstock; p.100 (4): Brandon Seidel/Shutterstock; p.100 (5): 1stGallery/Shutterstock; p.100 (6): Denise Lett/Shutterstock; p.100 (7): imageBROKER/Alamy; p.100 (8): IxMaster/Shutterstock; p.100 (CL): Blend Images/Alamy; p.100 (CR), p.100 (BR): imageBROKER/Alamy; p.100 (BL): Alinute Silzeviciute/Shutterstock.

Commissioned photography by Gareth Boden: p.13 (BR), p.23 (BR), p.33 (BR), p.45 (BR), p.55 (BR), p.67 (BR), p.77 (BR), p.89 (BR), p.99 (BR); Jon Barlow: p.9 (T), p.11 (T), p.19 (T), p.19 (C), p.21 (T), p.28, p.31 (T), p.41 (T), p.43 (T), p.56 (T), p.56 (BR), p.61, p.62, p.71 (T), p.72 (TL), p.72 (TR), p.72 (BC), p.85, p.95 (B), p. 97 (T).

Our special thanks to the following for their kind help during location photography:

Everyone Active-Parkside Pool Cambridge, Queen Emma primary School

Front Cover photo by Lynne Gilbert/Getty Images